See the CACTUS

DANIELLE SHUSTERMAN

See the cactus.

See the cactus at night.

See the flowers.

At night, the cactus has flowers.

See the juice.

The juice is in the flowers.

See the bat.

At night, the bats come out.

The bats like the juice.

The bats go flower to flower.

See the fruit.

See the seeds in the fruit.

See the wolf.

The wolf eats the fruit.

The wolf poops.

The seed is in the poop.

The seed will be a cactus.

See the cactus grow.

Where the SAGUARO CACTUS Grows

←California

←Arizona

←Mexico

Location of Saguaros

Sonoran Desert

Growing Facts

The saguaro cactus grows in the Sonoran Desert in Mexico and the United States.

It can take 10 years for a saguaro to grow 2 inches.

After 70 years, the saguaro is about 6.5 feet tall and can start producing flowers.

When it's between 75 and 100 years old, the saguaro will be about 16 feet tall and can start to grow its first arm.

The saguaro can live for over 200 years and reach a height of 70 feet.

I can find these items in the picture using first letter sounds.

cactus

wolf

fruit

poop

POWER WORDS

How many can you read?

has   is   like

see   a

go

in   to

the

come   be

will   at